LIPSTICK

by
Faleeha Hassan

Transcendent Zero Press
Houston, Texas

Copyright © 2016 Faleeha Hassan.

PUBLISHED BY TRANSCENDENT ZERO PRESS
www.transcendentzeropress.org

All rights reserved. No part or parts of this book may be reproduced in any format, except for portions used in reviews, without the expressed written consent from the author or from the publisher.

ISBN-13: 978-0-9962704-7-2

ISBN-10: 0-9962704-7-7

Printed in the United States of America

Library of Congress Control Number: 2016959662

Cover design by Glynn Monroe Irby
Cover image taken from public domain: http://absfreepic.com/free-photos/download/many-of-lipstick-4304x2869_58243.html

FIRST EDITION
Transcendent Zero Press

LIPSTICK

by
Faleeha Hassan

Contents

We age at the speed of war / 9-11

If I didn't love you / 11

Let's Hate the Moon Together / 12-13

Little Moments / 14

I Give You the Shadow of a Flower / 15

If You Could Live So Far From Me / 15

Free Me From my Vows / 16

My Mother and Father / 17

I Wonder / 18

the Heart has a Dream to Protect / 18

Regaining my Life / 19

My Lover and I and other Animals / 20

Dilemma / 21

This May Not be a Poem / 21-22

Black Iraqi Woman / 23-24

Age / 25

Wish / 26

Longing / 26

The Child Martyr / 27

Stalingrad / 28-29

Just a place I care / 30

a place of exile / 31

Soldier / 31

Life Spans / 31

Me / 32

Just a Question / 32

What Interests Me / 33

Letters Obviously Not Intended for Anyone Else / 33

Another Question / 33

Talismanic Incantation / 34

Prayer / 35

The Futility of Protesting Near Bustling Cemeteries / 36

Two Doves / 37

What a wonderful world / 38

Short Poems / 39-40

Memory / 40

Be careful / 41

Troth 2 / 41

Parting / 41

Head / 42

If I was a poet / 43

A poem for you / 44

Regaining my life / 45

War game / 46

Windows or Days / 47

At the Margin of The War / 48-49

Writer's Block / 50-51

Iraqi Haikou / 52-53

Let's Strongly Celebrate My Day / 54-55

Lipstick / 56-57

Cesspool Your Name is War / 58

Lament / 59

A Southerner / 60-61

Not Maryam / 62-64

NOTES / 67-69

We age at the speed of war

God never asked us when he threw his warning
by saying: become. We were children stuttering
in the whispers of sleeping homes.

We ran to schools surrounded by our mothers'
prayers that feared everything.
But the head mistress shortened our lives with a quiet sentence:
'we'll return after the end of the war… in 10 days only',
in her Kurdish accent.

So we, the students, remained, gathered in the school yard
Wide eyed, our souls bewildered and afraid.
the days stretched and became years;
we separated. The sons to the battleground
and the girls to the waiting steps.

my friends never returned.
their leftovers were gathered in wooden boxes
decorated with holes of separation.

my mother, like us, suffered from waiting;
she sat beside us awaiting my father,
who used to return a time and leave many times;
we didn't know where he went.

To avoid a question he'd say: to the mobile frontline.
we started to collect our days and stuff them in calendars.
In our grief we painted our eyes with the dust
of graveyards. There was nothing but the banners
(long live the leader).

and yes, he lived long enough to stitch one war with another.
my father's sister counts her children with her days
they never returned.
In one wake she said goodbye
to all of them
then vowed for a long silence.

'we left the war as winners'
hah

the leader said
'lets go to my second war'
the soldiers knew nothing about it.

my mother counts my brother's soldier belts,
she knows the battles are a loosing game.

we hunger.
we hunger,
as the leader's belly grows.

He appears, crying on the channels;
'I only have one suit',
And behind the screen, he marries his son in a golden aeroplane.

'Don't worry'

My neighbour pats his son's back,
'I returned from the war alive and will stay.'
He rushes before the light of dawn to the hospitals
And the pennies in his veins he invested.

my sister sits,
putting her baby to sleep, she sings: 'I want the war to never return,
And you stay for me.
make up for your father who left us without rerun.
The martyr of wars.'

But she's bad,
A hypocrite;
So crafty;
she eavesdrops, and as soon as he grows she steals him.
'Don't you have enough?'

Will there be a day that I can surround my family
with quiet – like other people?

Will there be a day that I count my wishes
in a notepad and they come true?

I am no woman if I don't speak to you face to face.
And this gesture does not suit you.
You are but the worst free spirit.

If I didn't love you

Far from the possibility of my death
– Like the rest of humankind –
When the body becomes compost for a tree,
Some of it may attach to the wheels of a car,
Or a bird may feel greed for a piece of meet
And it leaps with its beak toward me…

Or street cleaners could sweep it along
And I become as good as abandoned debris,

Or even be struck by a broom for a pile to burn,
I say:
Far from thoughts that grow in the pathways
Of the head, if I didn't find you
Would I have survived?

Let's Hate the Moon Together

Between two wars you came.
You mediated
And lit the fire of a new love.

And we began to spread ourselves between two suns
One for me
And the other for your eyes when the roads vanished.
We only fell out over the A,
When it wanted to insert itself
Between the W and R.

We told each other I love you.
The wars are made beautiful with songs
Which wipe the blood from the wars' lips.

We're never far from its grip.
We can exchange with it our stay
And I was as I always was
Loving your letters and always seek them.

So you, my soul mate,
You, the voice of my voice,
You, the dotting and un-dotting of my letters
the teacher said:
'You'll remove my sorrows
and return a tenderness to my soul.'
And you said:
'I will make flowers of you.'

I had forgotten the greenness of an evening,
after the drought of my femininity.

Return to me then
So that we can hate this informer,
This idiot.
His image is like a blonde
Forgotten by the aged.

We forget that our sky is black
despite his existence,

And it is red despite his clinging
to the tails of a dubious morning's veil.
Come back
So we can hate him.
This traitor,
Over the uniformed streets he looms
Like a policeman watching
My fingertips and your fingertips.

Come back again,
So I can show you my essence
Like the pages of your notebook.
Come back to me then,

So I can tell the apples in the basket
Like they told me about you.

Little Moments

I love the dove
She motions alone.
I curse her
She gets sold and returned.

A moment without your voice,
The essence of silence.
A moment without seeing you,
Complete blindness.
A moment without you,
Utter futility.
But…
Would you die of the cold?
I die from a dab of cold
And a lie,
Just like the dove.

I Give You the Shadow of a Flower

Cling to me.
Alone, you cannot lead you to yourself.
Cling to me,
My lost twin.

Your ah refuses to sound like Allah
We're not in the desert,
Waves have not deluged us
And the wind's fingernails are far.

But if loneliness reaches you,
The soul becomes dry
And all names loose their meaning.

Cling to me,
Only
To know the meaning of things.

If You Could Live So Far From Me

Do it
If you could strain from the cloud of the soul
Some cleansing water,
And turn the rusting dust of today
Into bunches of hope
Do it.
And if you could see in the mirror
Someone else's shrapnel,
Do it.
Yes.
Do it.
Live from my absence,
If you could live so far from me.

Free Me From my Vows

When longing becomes madness
And everything is silent except my heart,

I tiptoe in fear that my eyes may see me
Toward clothes
Omitted by anger toward you.

I brush off them the dust of desire.
I smell them
Searching for your dew
Or a drop of your scent.

I press between the muscles of your shirt
To quiet my pains
And regain the balance of my soul

So free me from my vows
Because I often do this.

My Mother and Father

My innocence nudges me
as she points to the creases of my bedding on the ground.

While the bed itself, with the imbecility of its sheets,
lies rejected in the corner of the room.

My parents' smiles widen with the stupidity of the covers.

They alone, and the bed
proved to me my innocence and the idiocy of a tidy bed.

Even if I inherited the furniture, children
And the creases under the eyes,

Every time my bed rubs in the carpet's weave,
I am still baffled by the wideness of their smiles,

As I lie between my children
On a stupid, tidy bed.

I Wonder

Even if I wasn't born in a house
That needed a home to complete it,
I would have been a …
Or …
Or …
But there's only poetry in the heart of a poet.

the Heart has a Dream to Protect

Tell me a word
Or a letter.
Begin the sound of a vowel and leave the rest to me.
Yes.
Do not take on a silence,
It makes me the world's oldest orphan.

Regaining my Life

Right under the tap, I put my head
And I turn the handle above.

In the running water
There are the sticky words of my boyfriend,
The barking of the street,
The creases of the rugged days,
Histories I bite with anxiety,
And cities that don't resemble
The silk of our poems.

The words pour
Like hair dyes that cover gray into the bathroom drain.
And in a while
I lift my head
As if I had not been strangled,
A few minutes ago,
By his hands.

My Lover and I and other Animals

Like two puppies,
When I see him
We sniff one another.
Like cats
We lick the fingers of our desire.

With the eyes of a wolf, he watches
for any movement near me.

He becomes a tiger
With rage
But I,
Like the hungry chick of a bird
I anticipate him.

Dilemma

I think of you and my shoes a lot.
How will I meet you
In a broken heel
Like my rotten luck?

This May Not be a Poem

Don't write my name here,
This may not be a poem.
Just take the coal and burn our red present tense.
Burn it well.
Throw its ashes far from the eyes of children.
Leave the Imra'u El Qais* - thief of virgin's dresses -
As he unreels and runs away on his horse,
mocking what we have harvested
of a history that sticks to our backs.
Abandon the Rocks of Bani Aabbas*;
it is filled with flies that gathered from the stench of waiting.
The Umayyads* are illiterate.
Don't trip up on their letters, abandoned on the paths of heresy.
Don't trust dollars of the Abbasid prince,
It is faked by the Barmakids*.
And no, the Andalusians did not plant an orchard.
Only the Tatar* built a history that still repeats today:
Red – sanguineous.
Never swear again by the River Tigris,
Its age has shortened,
and our Euphrates has flooded with drought
and corpses.
Tear out this page if you like;
I might meet one who belongs more in history than myself.

And
Don't write my name on it
Because this might not be a poem,

But
Let or children cleanse themselves
From the filth of war and let them choose
For us new names.

……………………………………..

* *Imra'u El Qais: was a poet in the 6th century. He was known to love drinking and chasing women.*

* *Rocks of Bani Aabbas: are two rocks in Saudi Arabia, where the ancient poet, Antara Bin Shaddad, was said to meet his lover. He tied his horse to one rock and hid by the other, waiting for her.*

* *The Umayyads Caliphates: was a dynasty that ruled after the death of the Prophet Mohammed.*

* *The Barmakids: they ruled under the Abbasid Caliphates of Baghdad.*
The Tatars: are the Mongols who invaded Baghdad in 1258.

Black Iraqi Woman

Shortly before my father died, he whispered to me longingly: "Daughter, treasure this, because it authenticates your heritage to our kinsfolk!" When I accepted this object, I discovered it was a stone with inscriptions I did not understand and delicate, mysterious lines. He continued, "It is a keepsake from our great-great grandfather and can ultimately be traced back to Bilal, the Holy Prophet's first muezzin, and his father, who was the king of Ethiopia." I accepted this small heirloom, which I carried everywhere with me in my handbag. The person who shared my life under the title of "husband," however, threw it down the drain at our house, thinking—as he told me—that it was a fetish. From then till now I have endured successive exiles. So I wrote this poem to explain the secret of my skin colour—given that I am a native of al-Najaf, Iraq—spiritually, mournfully, and poetically!

My father said: "You were born quite unexpectedly,
Remote from Aksum, like a beauty spot for al-Najaf—
'the Virgin's Cheek.'
Your one obsession has been writing, but
The sea will run dry before you arrive at the meaning of meaning."
He affirmed: "During a pressing famine,
I devoted myself to watching over every breath you took.
I would thrust my hand through the film of hope
To caress your spirit with bread.
You would burp, and
I would delightedly endure my hunger and fall asleep.
I could only find the strength to fib to your face and say I was happy.
I would feel devastated when you fidgeted,
Because you would always head toward me,
And I felt helpless."
Aksum! They say you're far away!
"No, it's closer to you than your exile."
"And now?"
"Don't talk about 'now' while we're living it."
"The future depresses me. How can I proceed?"
How can the ear be deaf to the wailing from the streets?
Aksum, you have coloured my skin. Al-Najaf has freshened my spirit.
She knows and does the opposite.

She knows that I inter only dirt above me, and
That I deny everything except spelling out words:
M: Mother, who went walking down the alley of no return.
F: Father, who hastened after her.
B: Brother, who never earned that title.
S: Sister who buttoned her breast to a loving tear, no matter how fake.
.....................There's no one I care about!
The trees tremble sometimes, and we don't ask why.
My life surrounds me the way prison walls surround suspects;
I am the victim of a building erected by a frightened man.
With its talons time scratches its tales on me,
And I transform them into a silent song
Or, occasionally, a psalm of sobs.
Father, do you believe that—the roots have been torn asunder?
Fantasies began to carry me from al-Najaf to Afyon
And from Afyon to nonexistence,
Yellow teeth stretching all the way.
"History's not anything you've made,"
One American neighbor tells another.
He's surprised to see me.
"Who are you?" he asks when he doesn't believe his eyes.
Would he understand the truth of my origin
If I told him I was born in al-Najaf
Or that Aksum has veiled my face?
I have walked and walked and walked.
I'm exhausted, Father.
Is your child mine?
Show yourself and return me to the purity of your loins.
Allow me to occupy the seventh vertebra of fantasy!
Don't eject me into a time I don't fit.
I need you.
I ask you:
Has my Lord forbidden me to be happy?
Am I forbidden to preserve
What I have left
And sit some warm evening
Averting my ear from a voice that doesn't interest me?
Answer me, Father!
Or change the face of our garden
So it changes . . .to what they believe!

Age

I part my days:
One half for daughters not able yet
To count by hand
Or walk with open heart,
And a half for the man huddling upon the age
As heavy as the war
Or, like a palm with no breath of odor.
What left I turn to birds
Replete with white…
Fleeting sea gulls,
Butterflies lisping with magic,
Signs of Surprise,
Tales about elves,
And the carol
Living deep in the dream
Narrated by the grandma
As she was warning me
To run away
So that the core of the sea would cool off.
But, I forget her warning,
Wandering far out in my head,
But .. the clock calls to my dreams
So I come back…
To part my days:
One half for daughters not able yet
To jump as high as the wash rope
Burdened with woolen clothes,
And half
For the man sitting in silence
Away…
Sipping the nectar of the present
And cursing upon the future sorrow.

Wish

I'd like to come to you
But, our streets are red
And I do not have
But my white dress.

Longing

When the tomb has regained its lovely dimness,
I made my heart a window,
And started to praise my murderer.

The Child Martyr

For you, I write letters,
The others would be haunting me,
I hurried to the well to whisper:
It was a fast meeting
Like a bullet buried, through a bat, into the soldiers' ribs.
It was a slow meeting
Like a mother's tear
As she, preparing travel food
For the one born by the frontiers,
Whose birth certificate is full of worries.
All the overcoats are too large for him,
Yet, it is said that he's worn an overcoat,
This is doubtful,
For he's never been obsessed
With an instinct to take off his country.
I'll gather all those bloods
Still traveling…
Lest I should say that
Our descriptions are but kindred.
Some difference is there between us,
It is the wound, oh my companion,
To which I am an echo.

Stalingrad

During moments I yearned for forests grown for me alone,
Caressing them in a dream,
I could sense the throbbing of the heart
Hidden beneath my ribs to bless my journey.
Summoning me with a pulse that he recognizes in me.
I heard the noise of abandoned smoke from a moment of care
Join with me,
Forcefully traversing desires to the hidden-most one.
My spirit swung toward him,
Creating a tingling
On lips that devour breaths alive.
I felt ashamed,
But the eye,
In moments—I scarcely know what to call them—that took me on another route
Toward the television, saw warplanes . . . spray death on them.
At that moment,
The fire of machine guns raked all the bodies,
And another fire raked my body when I trained my eye on him
Hesitantly inclining his head
Toward a shoulder unaccustomed to the secret of the stars of war
Or to insomnia.
Oh . . . . I leaned on it!
And when he caressed a dumbfounded person
I felt his fingers like coiling embers inside me.
Bashfulness seized the excuse this caress gave . . . and vanished,
Eliminating distance till the two of us were one.
And the eye—he moaned: May love not forgive her the eye—
repeated another evasion

Toward a drizzle of men flung about in the air
by just the rustling of a pilot penetrating a building
To fall on screens as the debris of breaking news.

But his breaths ... shattering the still down of the cheek,
And turning their picture into mist as
Eddies of the screen's corpses . . . varieties of death
that they brought them.
The spirit that became a body,
The body that was sold for the sake of a touch,
The eye that was concealed in his image
And that approached the firebrand of conflagrations.
Everyone drawing close to everyone,
Everyone,
Everyone,
Everyone.
But the thunder of their machine guns splintered them:
Corpses piled on corpses,
I mean on me,
The eyes of those in it were extinguished.
They slept in a trench of silence.
My eyes' lids parted in a wakefulness obsessed with them.
I rose ... and embraced the chill
That the screens brought me in commemoration of Stalingrad.

Just a place I care

In the room of full death this
I taste my window, savor,
I eat my wall bread,
I drink my library water,
In the room of full death this
I am always Playing a game (I am alive).
Head,
In night
When I try to sleep,
So many thoughts jump in!
Big thoughts,
Tiny one,
Great thoughts,
Silly one,
Sensible thoughts, crazy one,

Pushing, kicking, fighting each other.
Oh. My God,
I hope I have a switch
Just
I turn it off
And everything will be quiet,
……
…….
…….
Oh …….I forget
I have the head of a poet.

a place of exile

Rip of my life,
My health,
My money,
And a lot of shoes!

Soldier

Don't dance on the Danube river,
It is filled with flies.
Don't smile to the flowers,
The flies come to them from the corpses left in the open air,
Don't look to the sky,
It is strangulated with smoke,
Just
Take off your dream from your head,
Close your eyes
And walk in the road,
The war wrote your name in the list of death.

Life Spans

I loved my grandmother,
But she devoted herself to the family.
I loved my mother,
But she devoted herself to my father.
I loved my father,
But he devoted himself to the war.

Me

Dawn hurts me.
Morning hurts me.
Afternoon hurts me.
Even night hurts me … and I say nothing.

Just a Question

Why do–
Whenever I open my window
On your smile–
You exude disappointment
Like a poem by Faleeha Hassan?

What Interests Me

I know there are men more tender than you
With eyes more protective than yours,
And more other things,
And . . . .
But I'm not interested in the number of hydrogen bonds
in molecules of water.
All I know is that without water, I'll die of thirst
And I'm the same
Without you.

Letters Obviously Not Intended for Anyone Else

He said, "I love…"
And fell silent,
As if "you"
Were a word best left unspoken.

Another Question

How can I eulogize myself for you
Once I am dead?
Isn't it enough that out of me you produce another me,
From you another you,
And from us other people?
Isn't it enough
That the sky isn't big enough for all the stars,
When we're together?

Talismanic Incantation

I gathered the pores of my being
And came to perfume them with your own fragrance
Only to discover that you are an oleander—a rosebay
While in the memory of unease and apprehension
I trace some features that resemble no one but you
An image has its own dimensions
And, when hopelessness assails me, I have roads
That never cease to pull and lead me toward you
And while in the nook of anxiety
I fancy a preordained timing
For events that never materialize
The image draws near
And I talk to it
About the tons of heavy separation
That oppress the seasons of my life
I have recited you as rain
Yet your lightning never came near me
Alienation gathered thick
Tears heaved with gushing flow
Who will tell you that
My silence is like the mouth of a volcano
I am boundless
Yet fettered only by my own memory
And you are
And will always be
The ever-never closest to me

Prayer

I beg You, God,
Help us:
We who are children just turned forty,
We who still don't know how to shake the gooey skin
from our pithy words.
We haven't wandered aimlessly with a dog
Merely
Because our grandfathers' bones have been filling the cemeteries
that our streets demand.
We haven't drunk coffee,
Because the noise of their artillery really didn't allow us to sleep.
Please, God,
When you are nigh, we shouldn't dream of sheltering under blankets;
We want to see no matter what You have in mind for us
I beg You!
Don't make matters go from bad to worse!
We're still kids—
Forever.

The Futility of Protesting Near Bustling Cemeteries

For the Most Important Person in My Life, My Son Ahmad

Preamble
Take my spirit for your shirt
And use my heart's arteries for shoelaces.

Poem
My spirit patched with raw dreams,
My soft body blemished by war's scars,
My heart crushed and crunched like
Leaves under foot—
These are the sole signs of my existence
In a room that awaits a hurricane
That dreams of unleashing its gales.

My son,
Let me say tonight,
Objectively,
That I can't do anything more.
What happens,
Happens all the time.
What doesn't happen,
Never happens,
But we always paint a comely face
On life's hideous visage.

Two Doves

Every time my father is late from the Battlefront
Sickness strikes my mother
and I tour with her the hospitals of Najaf.

I write to him come 'back to us now,
Make your sergeant to read my words: I am about to die'.

He returns my letter, laughing:
'We are the amusement of the blind man'.
Oh you River of Jasim, you tore my years
between my father's supposed victories
and my mother's wishes in the emergency room;

they used to take care to plant hope in her mind
by sticking on the glass door,
two notices that say: (awaiting death certificate).

Her heart ages so fast
I vomit from hearing the chants.
Every time the presenter says 'victory is on the horizon',

My grandmothers' eyes rise to the ceiling,
she hides a mocking smile.

With rage I scream at the screen 'no victory's coming'.

She whispers: 'god is generous'.
'You sound like my father when I asked for a new toy'.
She quietens and we contend,
Awaiting his return before a new battle.

Fearing that a last fight can end the life of a dove.
…………………..

*Najaf: an Iraqi city, where the poet was born and lived most of her life.

*River Jasim: is a river situated between Iraq and Iraq, the location of many battles during the Iraq/Iran war.

What a wonderful world

When on November nights
I place my arm
I try to ignore the piece of cardboard spread beneath me
The holes in my pants
My empty pockets
My gray hair which matches with my beard
My voice that echoes like an empty bowl
The yellow leaves covering me now
And the kicks of joggers
Who try to roll me off the sidewalk
I try to forget all these
Even my own stink
So I can remember Louis Armstrong singing
"What a Wonderful World "!

Short poems :

*Thief
A sea stole my tears
There for became large!

*me
The sun is like me
Alone
And burns !

*Him
It was necessary for him to die
In order to find an empty place for his body!

*Prayer neck :
Dear cord
When wrapped around me
Please be smooth
And fluffy
Like my a dream !

*why ?!
Your voice is just ordinary
Very ordinary
Why should my soul melt
Whenever I hear you whispering ?!

*truth
From the room overlooking the face of graves
I thought of a future of the Arabic Homeland!

*Similarity
I know the meaning of Similarity between
 (politics) and (onion)
Both of them raise tears !

*love sizzle
You, I
And gardenia flower with me
I think we are more than three!

Memory

I remember
I was born there
Near the dream
I was the only one in orphanage,
My mom was the only one to show us love,
In the morning
She back to the nature of eyes
and raining passion,
And when she sleeps
We still quiver
Like a washed dress in the wind.

Be careful

Be careful
When you place a clock on the wall
    Be careful
Do not make it fall
The seconds can sink you in loneliness!

Troth 2

When I go up my house stairs
 I ask it sadly
All of this climb you own, and there is someone who tramples on you?

Parting

At least
you will respect my feet
which ran to you in the way of longing
quickly,

At least
you will respect my forefinger
pressed gently on your door bell,
At least
you will respect my eyes
that stared at your closed door long
before you opened it
Yeah
Respect them
before you teach me
how I spell a word (parting)

Head

In night
When I try to sleep,
So many thoughts jump in my head
Big thoughts,
Tiny one,
Great thoughts,
Silly one,
Sensible thoughts, crazy one,
Pushing, kicking, fighting each other.
Oh. My God,
I hope I have switch
Just
I turn off it
And every think will be quiet,
……
…….
…….
Oh …….I forget
I have the head of a poet.

If I was a poet

I would have sneaked
In from the pores of a net.

I would have wrapped you in a prose
Poem that lacks precision and laid you to sleep
Under the covers of my bed.
Quietly.

So if love was to engulf me
And a longing rises from my soul
I would stretch the fingers of my hand towards
you and dabble with the words of the poem,
Letter by letter.

If I was truly a poet
I would have limped to the Lord by now
And sat by the foot of his throne
And held on to it
With both hands
And whispered: 'you are the Greatest,
most Beautiful, most Wonderful and Capable,
Will you create a lover for me?'

I mean only for me.

But I know
That my prayer will not be answered
Not because it is impossible.
More than that really,
Since I have never known
A man
Who has never betrayed his lover.

A poem for you

Just sit by my side here
Talk to me about the tree,
Don't think of food
I'm not hungry
Give the flower to this little girl
Your smile is enough for me
Don't look at the window
It is stormy.
Keep looking in my eyes
You feel peace.
Don't say :- " you look tired",
Life is harsh
But I'm trying to be optimistic
So I didn't write about
The war, fear, grief, parting, loss , disease, cold, purgatory,
Pain, suffering, cruelty, loneliness,
No,
I didn't write about all of these things
I just wrote a poem about you!

Regaining my Life

Right under the tap, I put my head
And I turn the handle above.
In the running water
There are the sticky words of my boyfriend,
The barking of the street,
The creases of the rugged days,
Histories I bite with anxiety,
And cities that don't resemble
The silk of our poems.
The words pour
Like hair dyes that cover gray in the bathroom drain.
And in a while
I lift my head
As if I had not been strangled
A few minutes ago,
By his hands.

War game

Yesterday we were kids
And we played a game with tow rope in the afternoon,
But we did not know
The war sitting behind our age
would weave a rope of death to play a game dragging men.

Windows or Days

On the demolished days of the south
The windows occupy us
Our narrow windows, like the heads of kings
We, who are delighted with what escaped from this life,
Become trees —it becomes ash
Before our eyes
The beggar sharpens
A dagger of eternal questions
When we become hungry
The heads take the shape of question marks
And we buy the lottery of prayers
We hold onto the beard of patience for a long time,
Our suitable charm for all kinds of weather
Each time the waves became inflamed
We burnt the silence in our forests
Trying to catch the black glow that was flowing
Out of the stone of desire

Maybe in the bleeding wind
In the air, standing still on the white
We will see our candle decorated
With roads

We are stuck in mire up to the bones, with the sermons
Our stretched eyes up to the gates of the palace
Dreaming of the throne
When the night becomes pitch black
It laughs at our reasonable wishes

Our names are delusions
Our life is a worry
Our distinctive marks, without mouths
We stare

At The Margin of The War

"Those are stars,"
 says the child,
 as airplanes distort the face of the sky.
"I used to rest my head,"
 his sister says, "upon his kind arms.
 I don't remember how we
 found the bones of the murdered one
 who was my Daddy who
 was defending us on this mirage-earth,
 asking a shadow; how did this begin?"

 The ash women cry,
"These are the portents of those lost
 in the darkness of the prisons."
 One of them calls for help,
"I didn't find him.
 He left without a helmet,
 and nothing distinguishes him
 but his heart.
 He was like my country
 too great to bear.
 They returned many corpses
 but not his."
"These are the marks of a faded morning,"
 says the woman who, still
 tidying the bed blankets,
 dreams he may come in one longing night,
 lights a match,
 holds back grief.

"These are the memories of past years,"
 says one who has just come.
"To whom has my age been sold as wood fire
 for a fire that has raged for twenty-three years
 without ending?
 These are mirrors for my hollow life."

Birds cry as they follow an Apache squadron,
"Where are the windows?
Where are the windows?
We want air!"

Writer's Block

When I try to write
I sense that millions of readers are
Crowding the paper's edge,
Kneeling, genuflecting, and lifting their hands
To pray for my poem's safe arrival.
The moment it looms on my imagination's horizon,
Gazing at the concept in a diaphanous gown of metaphor,
Young people smack their lips—craving double entendres.
Meanwhile, with piercing glances, the elderly scrutinize
Its juxtapositions and puns.
Then the concept smiles shyly, dazed at seeing them.
On the paper's lines both young and old meet for a discussion,
But my words resist
And erect walls of critical theories.
Then the paths of personal confession contract,
Contract,
Contract.
My imagination calmly shuts down,
And the conception retreats inside my head.
At that hour, it afflicts my world with
Bouts of destruction.
Workers refuse their paychecks.
Farmer let their fields go fallow.
Women stop chatting.
Pregnant mothers refuse to deliver their babies.
Children collect their holiday presents but
Toss them on the interstate.
Our rulers detest their positions.
Kings sell their crowns at yard sales.
Geography teachers rend their world map
And throw it in the waste basket.
Grammar teachers hide vowel marks in the drop ceiling
And break caesura by striking the blackboard.
Flour sacks split themselves open, and the flour mixes with dirt.
Birds smash their wings and stop flying.
Mice swarm into the mouths of hungry cats.
Currency sells itself at public auctions.
The streets carry off their asphalt under their arms
And flee to the nearest desert.

Time forgets to strike the hour.
The sea becomes furious at the wave
And leaves the fish stuck headfirst in the mud.
The shivering moon hides its body in the night's cloak.
Rainstorms congeal in the womb of the clouds.
The July sun hides in holes in the ozone layer,
Allowing ice to form on its beard and scalp.
Skyscrapers beat their heads against the walls,
Terrified by the calamity.
Cities dwindle in size till they enter the needle's eye.
Mountains tumble against each other.
My room squeezes in upon me, and
The ceiling conspires against me with
The walls,
The chair,
The table,
The fan,
The floor,
Glass in the frame,
The windows,
Its curtains,
My clothes, and
My breaths.
The world's clarity is roiled.
Atomic units change.
I vanish into seclusion,
Trailing behind me tattered moans and
Allowing my pen to slay itself on the white paper.

Iraqi Haikou

- A child is crying
His mom breast is cut
The losing battle !

- Dogs eating corpses
We are starving now
The face of blood!

- Tanks are destroying the streets
Our soldiers without weapons
The smell of ach!

- A river is drying
Women are crying
The voice of crow !

- Birds are migrating
Children are trembling
The sound of hunger!

- Homes are burn
War is back
It is emptiness!

- Cats are disappear
Civilization is collapses
The voice of siren

- Corpses are fills trucks
Women sweep the shard of glass
It is thunder!

- Streets are dirking
No treatment in hospitals
The fell of death!

- Planes are explode
My grandmother is died
The feeling of cold!

- Nightmare haunt me
Old man lost his leg
The eyes of horror !

Let's Strongly Celebrate My Day

I'm in my seventies-
Ms. Faleeha, as they call me.
I have decided
To celebrate my day.
I'll invite all my close friends to the party
Since I have many.
……………………………………
……………………………………
………………
I'll send invitations to the sea gulls at the beach
………
To the flowers grown on the sides of the roads,
………
To the running waves, those flatterers
Who, when I show up, hasten to kiss my toes again and again.
I'll invite the breeze; how much I love it though stricken with snowflakes,
My old friend, the bus
Which used to take me home from work,
……………
The other one, that was blue,
…………………
The flocks of ducks,
………………
The leaves of trees – those coming back home,
…………………
And my children's faces; all are here around me- as I imagine.
But, they seem busy now
With other things- more important.
What else? I asked myself.
Oh, yeah I remember …….
I'll write on a piece of paper:
"Let's celebrate it, it's my day."
But, I've not thought of ...
Who will make the cake, suffering I am from rheumatism,
I can hardly move.
Even If I can, what kind of a cake will it be
Without sugar or oil? I am on a diet.
And who will make the apple juice- I'm already run out of apples.

And Who will set the balloons
And fix them up to the ceiling?
And …..and …..and ?
Oh, I've got sick of all that.
I am, the so-called Faleeha, strongly willing
To celebrate alone by myself,
And thus, I'll embrace the computer and sleep.

Lipstick

A Babylonian once told me:
When my name bores me,
I throw it in the river
And return renewed!
* * * * * *
Basra* existed
Even before al-Sayyab* viewed its streets
Bathed in poetry
As verdant as
A poet's heart when her
Prince pauses trustfully to sing
While sublime maidens dance--
Brown like mud in the orchards
Soft like mud in the orchards
Scented with henna like mud in the orchards—
And a poem punctuates each of their pirouettes as
They walk straight to the river.
I've discovered no place in the city broader than Five Mile.
He declared:
I used to visit there night and day,
When sun and moon were locked in intimate embrace.
Then they quarreled.
The Gulf's water was sweet,
Each ship would unload its cargo,
And crew members enjoyed a bite of an apple
And some honey.
The women were radiant;
So men's necks swiveled each time ladies' shadows
Moved beneath the palms' fronds.
These women needed no adornment;

……………………………………………………………………..

Basra, also written Basrah is the capital of Basra Governorate, located on the Shatt al-Arab river in southern Iraq between Kuwait and Iran. It had an estimated population of 1.5 million of 2012. Basra is also Iraq's main port, although it does not have deep water access, which is handled at the port of Umm Qasr.

The city is part of the historic location of Sumer, the home of Sinbad the Sailor, and a proposed location of the Garden of Eden. It played an important role in early Islamic history and was built in 636 AD or 14 AH. It is Iraq's second largest and most populous city after Baghdad. Basra is consistently one of the hottest cities on the planet, with summer temperatures regularly exceeding 50 °C (122 °F)

* Badr Shakir al Sayyab (December 24, 1926 – 1964) was an Iraqi and Arab poet. Born in Jekor, a town south of Basra in Iraq, he was the eldest child of a date grower and shepherd. He graduated from the Higher teachers training college of Baghdad in 1948. Badr Shakir was dismissed from his teaching post for being a member of the Iraqi Communist Party. Badr Shakir al-Sayyab was one of the greatest poets in Arabic literature, whose experiments helped to change the course of modern Arabic poetry. At the end of the 1940s he launched, with Nazik al-Mala'ika, and shortly followed by 'Abd al-Wahhāb al-Bayātī and Shathel Taqa, the free verse movement and gave it credibility with the many fine poems he published in the fifties. These included the famous "Rain Song," which was instrumental in drawing attention to the use of myth in poetry. He revolutionized all the elements of the poem and wrote highly involved political and social poetry, along with many personal poems.

Cesspool Your Name is War

As they opened the gates of war,
My father have had to take off his youth
To go in stripped of hope of return,
And mom had lie in the bed of tears
Covered with her agony.
Only me was there,
Foolishly, watching the silent clock on the wall
As it strikes my disappointments, one by one.
Two wars had later passed, or more,
When father returned but as a flag,
Mother flapped, and both vanished high into the sky.
Since then our home has turned into a soldier's boot.
Whenever I try to dust it off,
A burnt memory would fall off a day
That'd been lost in the cesspool of war.
....

Lament

My city is the violated
Streets torn by desires
of the kingdom,
Despite our numbers
That surmount gold bullions
In the prince's room,
We fall as we walk
While our sheikh*
- God save his soul -
Thrived on our blood,
He spread the skins
To perform his prayers

....

*Sheikh: a revered old man, an Islamic scholar, an elder or the Wiseman of a tribe.

A Southerner

Oh I forgot.
The war that left us for two seconds
Yes, only two seconds, I forgot to throw a stone after it
- As my mother said.*

So it returned with all its might
and swallowed us whole.

A southerner;
Of shyness and apples
Wars grilled me on their fires.

No
I don't fear the beautiful face of war
The letters make me a liar
And paper whiteness mocks my words.

...

I am southerner.
Sadness grinds me to make the scents of sorrows.
And jaded by windowsills of houses where birds don't visit
I ask
When will my heart mature?

...

I am southerner.
I sleep little
And dream between one heartbeat and another
That a branch leans over
And asks: who will replace the art of spying by revealing identity?

A southerner,
I know the meaning of similes in politics
And the pungency of onions,
They both evoke my tears.

....

Of the old Iraqi traditions (that the Iraqis throw stones behind an unwanted or unwelcome guest if he left the house).

Not Maryam

Father, I am not Maryam.
Not Maryam.

Despite that
The one you see
Utter between you,
I am not his mother
And he is not borne from me
Yet the one called Jesus
belongs to me.

...

I am not Maryam, father
Not Maryam.

I buy my bread with my own tears
Every time
You don't feed me.

Your sky is grapes
And I have not a prophet's uncle
and My mother didn't sell me
For the Qibla* of her prayers.

Why then do I see the deaf
And blind
Fight me at my doorstep?

...

Not Maryam, father.
I am not Maryam.

I was not a sister to Harun*
My hands are my witnesses
They tire of shaking
the root of your palms

And I did not dream
of flour falling into my hands

The drink I brought
Is tasteful only to myself.

What's with these horses
Bleeding and whining
At my sight?

…

I am not Maryam, father.
I am not her.

Your women seek
me for the onset of labour.
And this face
Its features moulded
by the palm of the wind
is ruined by exile.

But I present myself
As a temple
Lest you claim
that I am Maryam.

For the first dawn
I do not rise to deceit,
I am not hanged -
and have no fear.

I am not Maryam, father
I am not Maryam.

....

* *Qibla: the direction that a Muslim faces when performing daily prayers.*

* *Harun: (Harun Al Rashid 766-809) His date of birth is debatable. The Thousand and One Nights tales were based on him and his imagination.*

NOTES

The poem ("Windows or Days") is translated by **Khaloud Al-Muttalibi**. She is a poet and translator living in the United Kingdom. Much of her work has been translated into Romanian, Punjabi, Spanish, and English. Her poetry, translation, and essays have appeared in a wide variety of literary journals. She has appeared in several books and anthologies. Her published works include *Psalms under a London Sky, Under an Icy Sky, A Portrait of Uruk* (an anthology of poems and stories) and *The Contemporary Iraqi Poetry Movement* (an anthology of poems). She has translated Arabic poems into English, for poets from countries such as Iraq, Algeria, Morocco, Palestine and Syria. She has also translated literary criticism articles. Khaloud has participated in *The Anthology of Contemporary Arabic Poetry* as a poet and a translator, published by the Artgate Association in Romania. She has also translated numerous Modern and classic English and American poems.

The poem ("At The Margin of The War") is translated by **Soheil Najm Hasis**. He published four books of poetry, *Breaking the Phrase* (1994), *Your Carpenter O Light* (2002), *No Paradise Outside the Window* (2008), and the anthology *Flowers in Flame* (2008). In addition, he has translated selections of work by Nikos Kazantzakis, Alasdair Gray, Ted Hughes, and José Saramago. Najm. He is currently the editor of the *Althaqafa Alajnabia* ["Foreign Culture"] journal in Baghdad. He participates courtesy of the Bureau of Educational and Cultural Affairs at the US Department of State.

The poem ("Talismanic Incantation") is translated by **Mahmoud Abbas Masoud**. He is a philosopher, writer, and translator.

The poems ("Age", "Wish", "Longing", "The Child Martyr", "Cesspool Your Name is War" and "Let's Strongly Celebrate My Day") are translated by **Hussein Nasser Jabr**. He is from Nasirriya, Iraq and has a University Degree M.A. in English and Linguistics. His literary career has been as a Poet and Translator of many important Arab writers. He produced an English translation of four poems by Faleeha Hassan, published in the Iraqi literary journal, *Gilgamesh*, in 2008. In addition, he translated a poem by her, entitled "The Child Martyr", published in a book of poetry entitled *Heart Fire: Second Revolutionary Poets Brigade Anthology* in 2013, and a collection of her poetry entitled *The Spark of Seeing You*.

The poems ("Black Iraqi Woman", "Stalingrad", "Life Spans", "Me", "Just a Question", "What Interests Me", "Another Question", "Letters Obviously Not Intended for Anyone Else", "Prayer", "Writer's Block", "Lipstick" and "The Futility of Protesting Near Bustling Cemeteries") are translated by **William Maynard Hutchins**, an American academic, author and translator of contemporary Arabic literature. He is currently a professor in the Department of Philosophy and Religion at Appalachian State University in Boone, North Carolina. He graduated from Yale University 1964, where he majored in art history. Hutchins in 1978 joined the faculty of I. Appalachian State. He was promoted to full professor in 1986. As a translator, Hutchins's best-known work is his translation of the *Cairo Trilogy* by Egyptian Nobel Prize winner Naguib Mahfouz. This trio of novels is widely regarded as one of the finest works of fiction in Arabic literature, and Hutchins' translation is the principal version available in English. In 2005-2006, Hutchins received a US National Endowment for the Arts grant in literary translation.

The poems ("If I Did Not Love You", "Let's Hate the Moon Together", "Little Moment", "I Give You the Shadow of a Flower", "If You", "Free Me from my Vows", "My Mother and Father", "I Wonder", "The Heart Has a Dream", "Regaining My Life", "My Lover and I", "Dilemma", "This May Not Be a Poem", "Two Doves", "We Grow Up in Speed of War", "Lament", "A Southerner", and "Not Maryam") are translated by **Dikra Ridha**, a writer, poet, and literary translator with an MA in Creative Writing from Bath Spa University. A collection of her poems was published in a pamphlet entitled 'There are no Americans in Baghdad's Bird Market' by Tall-lighthouse, 2009. Dikra translates poetry between Arabic and English and has been teaching Arabic Language at the University of Bath and private lessons. Her new children's picture book, *Leo and The Sleep Fairy* was released in December 2014 and she is currently translating it into Arabic. Dikra is also preparing a collection of poems on exile, family love, and culture shock.

The poems ("Soldier", "What a Wonderful World", "Short Poems", "Head", "War Game", "a place of exile", "Iraqi Haikou", "Just A Place I Care") are written by **Faleeha Hassan** in English directly is poet, writer, playwright, author of short stories, novels and children's books. She fled her country because her voice could not be stilled. She grew up knowing the tribulations of war for most of her life and she has personally witnessed many of the horrible things perpetrated by her countrymen against her family and her fellow citizens. Yet, she still brings a breath of fresh air with her clever way of weaving the words in a foreign language (to her) - English that crosses political, religious and language boundaries. She has that rare capacity to connect her words with something that is inside of all of us that resonates with her descriptions. Her words are powerful reminders, that it echoes in your head full of meaning regardless what language it is translated.

www.ingramcontent.com/pod-product-compliance
Lightning Source LLC
Chambersburg PA
CBHW022124040426
42450CB00006B/843